THE HUMMINGBIRD BOOK AND FEEDERS

By Neil Dawe • Illustrated by Jock MacRae

Diagrams by Margo Davies Leclair

SOMERVILLE HOUSE, USA

Contents

- **4** Feathered Jewels
- **6** What's a Hummingbird?
- **8** Feathers
- **10** Hovering Flight
- **12** Feeding and Diet
- **14** Territory
- **16** Courtship Displays and Mating
- **20** Nest Building, Eggs, and Young
- **22** Migration
- **24** Torpor

Your Hummingbird Feeders

- **26** Creating the Hummingbird Nectar
- **27** Filling the Feeders
- **28** Setting Up Your Feeders
- **30** Cleaning the Feeders
- **31** Why Aren't Hummingbirds Coming to My Feeders?

Hummingbird Projects

- **32** Document Your Hummingbirds' Arrival
- **32** Provide Nesting Materials for Your Hummers
- **33** How Do Hummingbirds Control Their Temperatures?
- **34** Plant a Hummingbird Garden

☞ **Flip the pages of the book to see the hummingbird hover.**

Feeder Experiments
- 36 Instructions
- 38 Experiment Charts
- 39 Do Hummingbirds Have a Favorite Color?
- 40 Can Hummingbirds Learn?
- 40 How Sweet Do Hummingbirds Like Their Nectar?

Field Guide
- 42 Identifying Hummingbirds
- 44 Ruby-throated Hummingbird
- 45 Black-chinned Hummingbird
- 46 Costa's Hummingbird
- 47 Anna's Hummingbird
- 48 Calliope Hummingbird
- 49 Broad-tailed Hummingbird
- 50 Rufous Hummingbird
- 51 Allen's Hummingbird
- 52 Southwestern Hummingbirds
- 53 Broad-billed Hummingbird
- 53 White-eared Hummingbird
- 54 Violet-crowned Hummingbird
- 54 Blue-throated Hummingbird
- 55 Magnificent Hummingbird
- 55 Lucifer Hummingbird
- 56 Scientific Names

DID YOU KNOW?

The Giant Hummingbird—the largest of the hummingbirds—can be up to 8 1/2 inches (21.6 cm) in length. The Cuban Bee Hummingbird—the tiniest bird in the world—is only 2 1/4 inches (5.7 cm) long from tip of bill to tip of tail.

Feathered Jewels

Hummingbirds! These little fireballs of energy zoom in and out of sight in the blink of an eye. Their feathers shimmer like jewels, and the buzz of their wings adds to the spring symphony as they move from flower to flower. Hummingbirds were given their name because of the sound their wings make. One close encounter and you'll hear why.

Hummingbirds are found in meadows, forests, deserts, and mountain lowlands in North, Central, and South America. They are one of the largest families of birds in the New World.

This book is all about hummingbirds. It will show you how to attract them and explain why you shouldn't feed them honey. You'll discover how fast their wings beat and how to tell the different kinds apart. You'll also learn how to do some simple experiments that will help you determine if hummingbirds have a

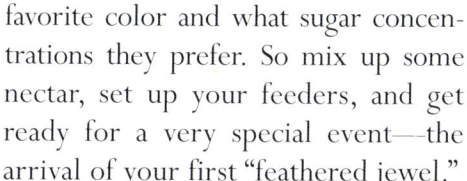

favorite color and what sugar concentrations they prefer. So mix up some nectar, set up your feeders, and get ready for a very special event—the arrival of your first "feathered jewel."

Hummingbirds need huge amounts of energy. If they're not hovering at flowers, feeding on nectar, they're probably perched somewhere, digesting the nectar they've recently gathered. [top] Lucifer Hummingbird [left] Anna's Hummingbird [right] Calliope Hummingbird

What's a Hummingbird?

What makes a hummingbird a hummingbird? How can hummingbirds do such amazing things? One reason is that their bodies have evolved in unusual ways. Here are some examples of how hummingbird bodies differ from those of most other birds.

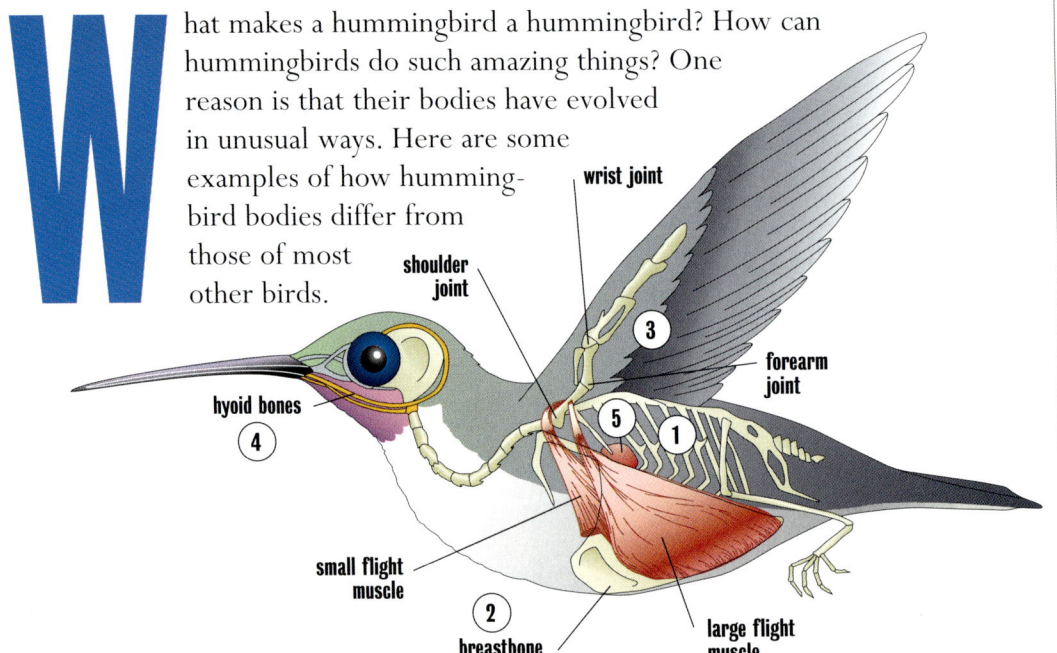

1 Hummingbirds have eight pairs of ribs to protect them from the rigors of their hovering and incredible dives. Most land birds have only six.

2 Hummingbirds have an enlarged breastbone that runs nearly the length of their bodies. It provides room for their extra-large flight muscles to be attached.

3 Hummer hands are long and the arms are short, as in other birds that depend on flapping flight. (Gliding flight requires a long arm and short hand.)

Because hummer wing bones remain rigidly outstretched during flight, the wrist and forearm joints aren't as flexible as those of most other birds, which bend their wings as they fly. Hummer wings are more like oars. They join at very flexible swivel-type shoulder joints.

4 Hummers have special elongated bones, called *hyoid bones,* that run from the back of the skull and attach to the tongue. When the bones are moved forward, they allow the tongue to extend considerably from the tip of the bill, enabling hummers to reach inside flowers for food.

5 Hummers have the largest hearts for their size and the fastest heart rates when they are active—up to an incredible 21 beats per second—of any bird. This gives hummers' bodies oxygen-rich blood and nutrients at a fast rate to supply the huge amount of energy the hummers need to hover.

Feathers

DID YOU KNOW?

The first birds evolved about 160 million years ago. Birds' feathers evolved from the scales of their reptilian ancestors, and birds still have scales on their legs and feet. Birds are the only animals with feathers.

Among the first things you notice about hummingbirds are the brilliant, iridescent colors of their feathers—reds, purples, blues, and greens. It is the adult male hummingbirds that have the most intensely colored feathers. The feathers of their throat area, or *gorget,* are often particularly dazzling. They may appear dark until the light strikes them at just the right angle, then flash with brilliant color. The feathers of female hummingbirds are less colorful. Unlike the males, females do not need ornaments for courtship display.

The colors in some of the hummingbird's feathers look iridescent because of the structure of the feathers. There are tiny trapped air bubbles in the feathers that *refract,* or bend, the light that hits them. The bubbles also reflect some of the light, like a mirror. Together, the reflection and refraction cause certain colors to be reinforced, while other colors interfere with each other and are canceled out, making the feathers look iridescent. Hummingbird colors can also appear when pigments in the feathers absorb some colors of the light and reflect the others that you end up seeing.

The feathers of many hummers, as they are affectionately called, hum or buzz as air rushes through them when the bird is in flight. These sounds differ from species to species. Some hummingbirds, such as the Broad-tailed, have wing tips with tiny notches in them that are used to produce the metallic buzzing sounds we hear. Others, such as the Rufous, have notches in their tail feathers.

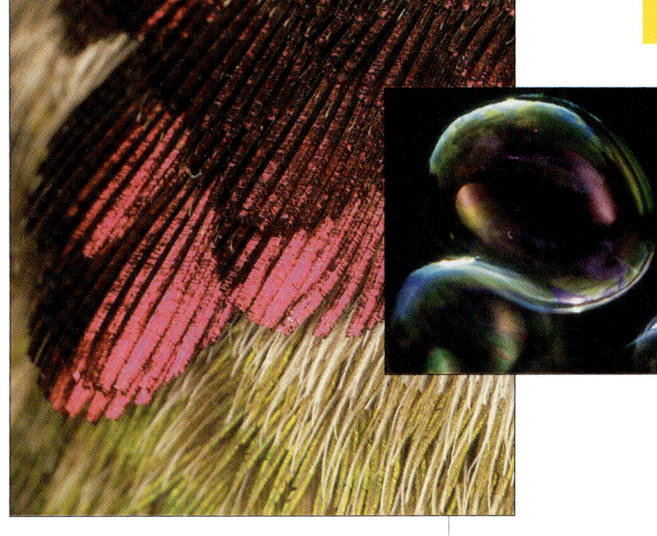

Like the sheen on a soap bubble, the iridescence of hummingbird feathers is caused by the reflection and refraction of light, in a process called *interference.*

DID YOU KNOW?

The smaller the bird, the faster the wingbeat. The male Ruby-throated Hummingbird's wings beat at the fantastic rates of 75 strokes per second during regular flight and up to 200 times per second in a display dive. In comparison, a chickadee beats its wings 30 times per second.

Hovering Flight

Hummingbirds are acrobatic flyers that cannot be matched by any other bird. Their tapered, compact wings are designed for rapid maneuvering, and their flight muscles are huge compared to their tiny size.

Birds have two pairs of flight muscles. A large muscle provides the powerful downstroke. A smaller muscle raises the wing. The flight muscles of strong flyers, such as falcons and swallows, can account for as much as one-quarter of the bird's total weight. A hummer's flight muscles can account for almost a third of its total weight! Its small flight muscles are much larger for its size than those of other birds and thus more powerful. Hummers also have very flexible shoulder joints that allow their wings to be flipped upside down. These two features enable the hummer to hover by rotating its wings in a figure-8 motion that, unlike the flapping of other birds, gains lift on the upstroke as well as the downstroke.

Hummingbirds can hover, fly straight up, and even fly backward and upside down.

To hover, a hummingbird holds itself at an angle, moves its wings forward, with its very flexible shoulder joints rotates the wings so that the undersides are facing up, brings the wings back, then flips them again to their original position. Each wing cycle, moving in a figure-8 pattern, takes just 1/500 of a second.

By tilting its body into a more horizontal position and changing the angle of the wings' figure-8 motion, the hummingbird can move slowly up to a flower or forward to feed.

As the hummingbird backs away from a flower, its body is nearly vertical, and its wing motion is slanted up and back.

The Hummingbird Book and Feeders

DID YOU KNOW?

Hummingbird hovering requires more energy than any other type of animal movement. Even a sprinter, running the 100-meter dash, uses less energy. Small hummers may eat up to five times their weight in nectar daily. For an 80-pound (36 kg) kid, that would be like eating 1,600 quarter-pound hamburgers a day.

Feeding and Diet

To eat, hummingbirds hover near a flower and reach inside with their needle-like bills for *nectar*. Nectar is the favorite food of many birds, but hummers are the best nectar gatherers by far. Their straight or downward curving bills are long and slender, and each species has a bill designed for feeding from flowers of a particular shape and size.

Hummer tongues, like those of woodpeckers, can extend far out from their bills. They can lap up nectar at a rate of 13 or more licks per second. The front half of the tongue is divided and has two grooves that act like a wick to draw in nectar. The tip of the tongue of some hummingbirds is often fringed, which may help to mop up nectar. Fringed tongues may also help hold the tiny insects found in flowers.

Insects picked from trees, shrubs, and flowers, and spiders captured at their webs, add protein to the hummer's diet.

Hummingbirds also swoop through swarms of flying insects, snapping them up with their bills as they go.

Hummers are about as small as a warm-blooded animal can be. If they were any smaller, they could not eat fast enough to stay warm. A hummingbird must feed many times each hour, throughout the day, to stay alive. It can visit nearly 3,000 blossoms a day. The nectar it eats is stored in its *crop*—a food storage area just before the stomach—then slowly released into its stomach. When the crop is half empty, the hummer feeds again.

Like all birds, hummers have sharp eyes, which they depend on to locate food—hummers have almost no sense of smell. They have excellent memories and will return daily and yearly to places rich with nectar-producing flowers.

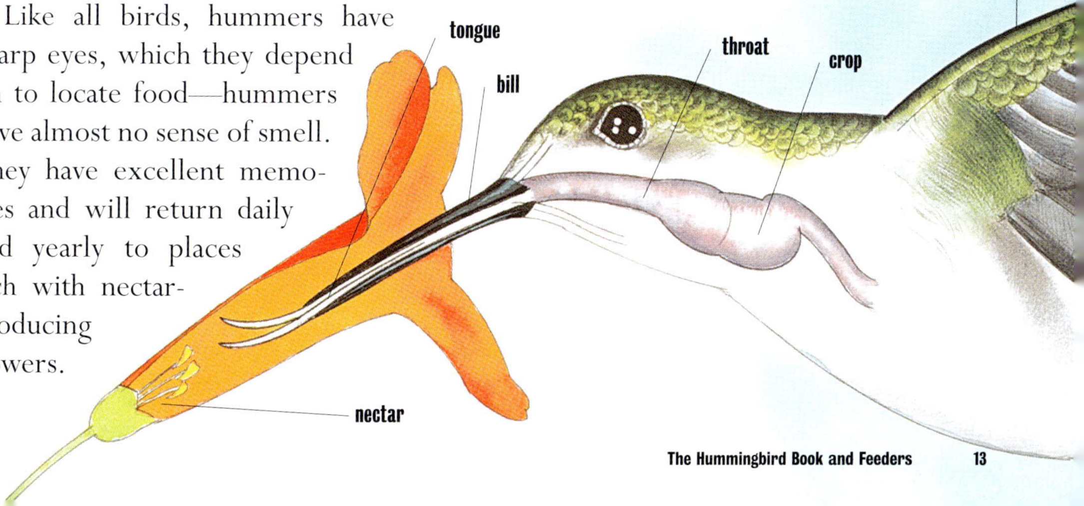

The Rufous Hummingbird feeds up to 15 times an hour, for about a minute at a time, storing nectar in its crop. It perches until the crop is half empty—this takes between three and four minutes—then feeds again.

Territory

DID YOU KNOW?

The male hummer's bright gorget effectively deters other birds from trespassing on its territory—at times, the gorget display is more effective than a chase.

Hummingbirds are pugnacious and aggressive. Flower patches that have an abundant supply of nectar are defended ferociously. A flower patch that is defended by a hummer is called its *territory*. Feeders can become a part of a hummer's territory, too.

How big is a hummer's territory? Well, that depends on how rich the nectar supply is and how many hummers are in the area! A dense patch of flowers in a small area can be enough to support

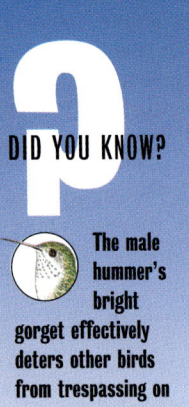

a hummer, but if the flowers are more scattered, the hummingbird will need to defend a larger area. And if there are lots of hummers around, it becomes difficult for a single hummer to defend a large territory because of the increased competition. In one case, a Costa's Hummer defended a territory containing 7,500 paintbrush flowers for a week—then was pushed off by a more aggressive Rufous Hummingbird.

Hummers will chase and attack other birds—including much larger birds such as jays, crows, and hawks—and insects that try to feed on the nectar in their territory. Hummers will even buzz cats and humans.

A Black-chinned Hummer dives on a Broad-tailed intruding into his territory. By eating little during the day, the defending male keeps his weight down. This lets him maneuver better and speed up faster than the intruder. Because they have no secure food source, intruders must feed heavily throughout the day.

DID YOU KNOW?

Birds communicate with each other by voice, actions, and the display of their feathers. Hummers' voices are not particularly musical, but their calls, made up of high-pitched, soft twitterings, squeaks, and chirps, can be extraordinarily complex.

Courtship Displays and Mating

Spectacular aerial dive displays are used by the male both to attract a female and defend his territory. The male hummer flies up into the air, sometimes as high as 150 feet (46 m), with his body angled so that his brilliant plumage glitters in the sun. He then dives rapidly toward the ground, reaching speeds of up to 70 miles per hour (113 km/hr) and pulling out of the dive at the last second. At the bottom of the dive, the bird may call or sing, or a loud metallic sound can often be heard. Scientists think this sound is generated by the tail feathers.

When the dive display is used during courtship, the female hummer is usually perched somewhere near the bottom of the dive. The display is often repeated six to eight times. A shuttle or whisking display is also used by the male to stop the female from flying away and appears to be more important than the dive display during courtship. This display usually

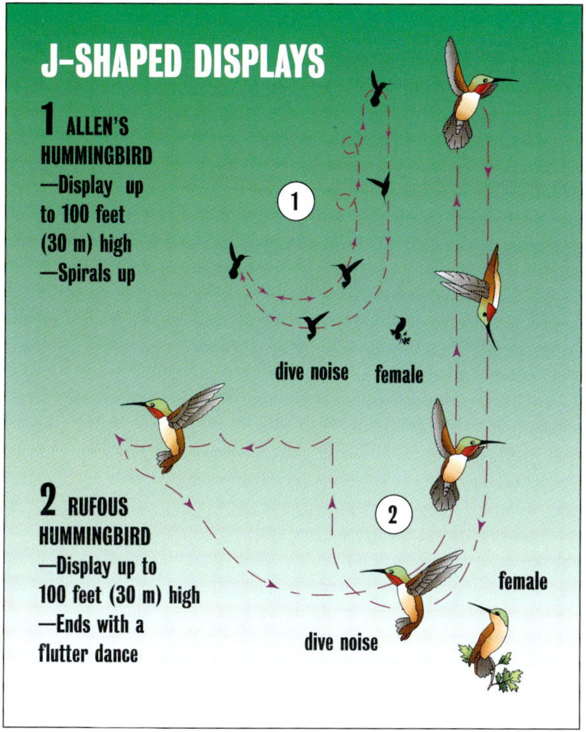

J-SHAPED DISPLAYS

1 ALLEN'S HUMMINGBIRD
—Display up to 100 feet (30 m) high
—Spirals up

dive noise female

2 RUFOUS HUMMINGBIRD
—Display up to 100 feet (30 m) high
—Ends with a flutter dance

female

dive noise

takes place amongst the shrubbery. The male flies back and forth 6 to 12 inches (15 to 30 cm) above the female, his wings making a whistling sound. The shuttle display is usually followed by a chase that ends with the male mating with the female. Mating has been reported in the air, on a branch, and on the ground.

The male hummer takes no part in nest building, incubating the eggs, or rearing the young, leaving the female to handle those tasks alone. Most male hummers breed with multiple females each season, and some females accept more than one mate.

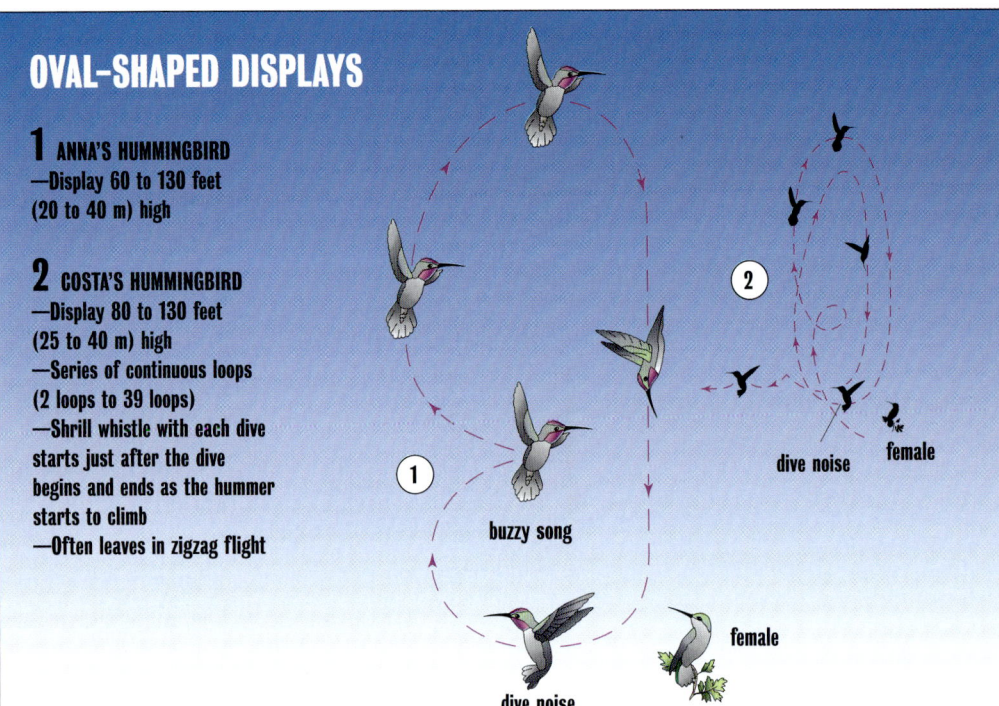

U-SHAPED DISPLAYS

1 RUBY-THROATED HUMMINGBIRD
—Display usually 8 to 10 feet (2.5 to 3 m) high, but as high as 30 to 50 feet (10 to 15 m)

BLACK-CHINNED HUMMINGBIRD
—Display usually 15 to 25 feet (4.5 to 7.5 m) high

2 CALLIOPE HUMMINGBIRD
—Display 30 to 90 feet (10 to 30 m) high
—Dive noise followed by a high, soft *bzzt*

BROAD-TAILED HUMMINGBIRD
—Display 30 to 60 feet (10 to 20 m) high
—Wing trill may be heard up to 245 ft (75 m) away

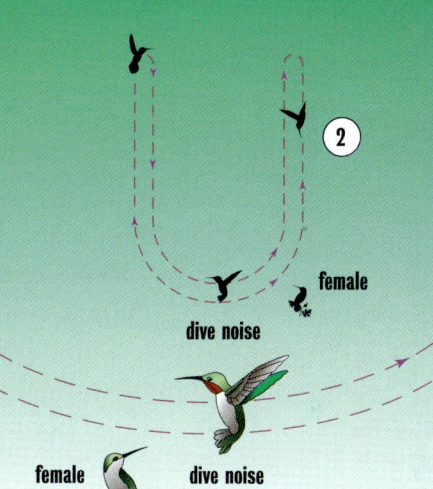

Nest Building, Eggs, and Young

Each hummingbird species makes a nest of unique design. North American hummers build tiny (around 1 1/2 inches [3.8 cm] wide), cup-shaped nests lined with soft materials such as plant down or animal fur, decked on the outside with bits of lichen or bark for camouflage. The nests are bound together with spiders' webs. They take from two to 10 days to construct.

After she completes her nest, the female lays her eggs—usually a set of two. Hummers face fewer hazards from predators and live longer than many birds—usually two or three years, but up to 12 years in the wild—so they don't need to lay as many eggs in order to maintain their numbers.

Hummingbird eggs are tiny—two could fit on a penny! But hummer eggs are huge compared to the mother bird, weighing from 10 to 20 percent of her weight. The eggs of most other birds weigh only about 2 to 4 percent of the female's weight.

DID YOU KNOW?

An Anna's Hummingbird's nest has the insulating quality of polar bear fur. The nest material helps keep the eggs and the female warm through the cold late-winter nights.

A female Ruby-throat feeds her young regurgitated nectar and insects that she pumps from her crop.

During *incubation,* the female must spend most of her time sitting on the eggs to keep them warm. She must also defend the nest against predators, maintain the nest, and manage to feed herself.

After about two weeks, the eggs hatch, and the mother starts feeding the tiny, helpless chicks—mainly on regurgitated insects. She *broods,* or warms, the chicks for the first 10 to 12 days. After about three weeks, the young *fledge,* or leave, the nest. The mother may remain with them for one or two weeks, but they soon begin to look for food on their own.

An ostrich egg could hold more than five thousand of the smallest hummer eggs.

Migration

DID YOU KNOW?

More than a third of the world's bird species—tens of billions of birds—migrate each year, but only a handful of the 340 hummer species are migrants. These include most of the species seen in North America.

One of the most amazing activities of birds is their *migrations*—great yearly round trips of hundreds or thousands of miles. Some hummers, such as the Costa's, migrate only short distances. Some, such as the Anna's, don't migrate at all. Others travel far north to reach new, less crowded habitats with more available food. The Rufous Hummingbird may fly up to 3,000 miles (4800 km) from its wintering grounds in Mexico to its breeding grounds in Alaska.

It takes millions of beats of the Ruby-throated Hummingbird's tiny wings to make the long, nonstop journey over the open waters of the Gulf of Mexico. Powerful wing muscles and fat reserves that serve as fuel enable the tiny Ruby-throats to achieve this incredible feat. Before setting off, they build up their fat reserves by feeding heavily on nectar and insects. Ruby-throats can double their body weight, all in a period of

one to two weeks, before they make the journey. Imagine having to eat so much before you go on a trip that you would weigh twice as much as you do now!

Migrating hummers, even the young, fly alone, stopping to feed when they find nectar-producing flowers, sleeping at night in a tree or shrub. If the weather is poor, or if the hummer finds a particularly good feeding spot, it will stop for a few days before resuming its journey.

How do migrating birds navigate so far so accurately? Scientists think that birds somehow inherit recognition of certain geographic features. They seem able to use celestial bodies (the Sun, the stars, and maybe the Moon) or the Earth's magnetic field to determine position and direction. They also have the capacity to learn by experience and remember migration routes.

Hummers, such as this Rufous, migrate alone. In some ways, their ability to find their way is more amazing than that of other birds that migrate in flocks and can use their group knowledge.

Torpor

DID YOU KNOW?

A resting hummingbird takes around 250 breaths per minute, a faster rate than all other birds. This supplies a large amount of oxygen to *oxidize*, or "burn," food quickly, releasing and converting the energy in the food to a form that the hummer can use.

Overnight, a hummer can lose 15 percent of its body weight, simply because it stops feeding. If people were like hummers, a 100-pound (45 kg) person could lose 15 pounds (7 kg) each night—just by going to bed. What, then, does a hummingbird do when it can't feed continuously?

Before a hummer roosts for the night, it feeds heavily throughout the day, turning the sugar in the nectar it eats into fat. The fat reserves and a crop full of nectar allow the hummer to remain alive through the cold night. On really cold nights, during bad weather, or when food is scarce, hummers have a special means of conserving energy—they go into a state called *torpor*.

When a hummer enters torpor, the rate at which it

burns food slows down, its breathing rate drops to between 14 and 6 breaths per minute, its temperature gradually lowers, and its heartbeat slows to around 50 beats per minute. Torpor may require as little as one-sixtieth of a hummingbird's awake—but resting—energy levels and a fifth of its sleeping energy levels. A torpid hummingbird can stop breathing for up to five minutes and appear lifeless! Hummers' ability to enter and exit torpor led to legends about their supernatural powers.

A hummingbird can remain in torpor for up to 14 hours. Some hummers may use torpor to prepare for migration—even if the weather is fine—to protect the extra energy reserves they have built up for the long journey. Because they are totally helpless in this state, however, hummingbirds are very reluctant to enter torpor and usually only use it as a last resort for survival.

The Anna's Hummingbird uses about five times more energy while hovering than while resting. When it is in a torpid state, it uses energy at a rate nearly 15 times *less* than its resting rate.

Your Hummingbird Feeders

Creating the Hummingbird Nectar

The nectar in flowers frequented by hummers has a sugar concentration of around one-fifth to one-quarter. We want to make a sugar-water mixture that mimics that nectar. Here's how:

1. Put 4 parts water and 1 part white *granulated* sugar in a pot and stir.
2. Bring the mixture to a full boil and continue boiling just until all the sugar has dissolved. (Boiling kills mold spores and bacteria, and helps reduce the amount of chemicals in the water.)

4 parts water

1 part white granulated sugar

3. Immediately remove the pot from the heat and turn off the stove.
4. Place a lid on the pot and allow the mixture to cool before pouring it into the feeders. Use a pitcher or funnel to pour.
5. Store any unused nectar solution in the refrigerator. It will

---

CAUTION!

Be sure to have an adult help you prepare the hummingbird nectar. Boiling sugar water can be very dangerous if spilled.

- **Use only white sugar. Do *not* use honey or artificial sweeteners. Honey can cause a fungal growth on the hummingbird's tongue that is fatal.**

keep well for about a week.

* There is no need to buy a commercial nectar mixture. Your hummers will get all the other nutrients they require from the flowers in your neighborhood.

Filling the Feeders

1. Separate the feeders by unscrewing the bolt and removing the connecting rod.

2. Pop off the clear containers, then slide apart the bases.

3. One feeder at a time, turn the container upside down and pour in the solution. Snap the base back on the container. Turn the feeder upright.

4. To make one big feeder, slide the four feeder bases together. (Press the container of the last feeder outward a bit.) Reattach the rod and bolt.

5. Wipe off any spilled sugar solution—it could attract unwanted insects.

Artificial sweeteners don't provide hummers with the calories required to meet their tremendous energy needs.

- **Do not add food coloring to the sugar solution. It can coat a hummer's tongue and interfere with its feeding.**

- **Do not boil the solution too long or it will become too concentrated. This will make the hummers thirsty.**

You can hang your feeders combined into a single unit...

Setting Up Your Feeders

Once you have filled your feeders, you need to find the right spot to hang them. Your hummingbird feeders are unique—together they form one large feeder! You'll use the four feeders separately for the experiments on pages 36 to 41. Otherwise, it's up to you whether you want to set up the four feeders in different locations or combine them into one big feeder.

• Put the feeders out early in the spring, when hummingbirds begin to arrive—as early as January or February in the South and as late as April or May in the North. If you live in an area where hummers occur year-round (such as the western United States and southwestern British Columbia), put your feeders up immediately, and hummers may visit them throughout the seasons.

• Place your feeders where both you and the hummers will see them easily. Good spots are near flowering plants or shrubs, in full sunlight. Once you have attracted some hummers, move the feeders to a permanent, shadier location sheltered from the wind. Direct sunlight causes the air and

solution inside the feeder to expand, and the feeders will tend to drip. Also, the sugar solution will spoil more quickly in warmer temperatures.

- Hang the feeders in the open, but near trees or shrubs that will provide the hummers with protective cover and suitable perches. In between feeding bouts, hummers like to rest.
- Hummers (except, perhaps, the Calliope Hummingbird) seem to prefer feeders that are fairly high with an open view all around.
- Place feeders where cats cannot reach them and where hummers will not fly into windowpanes during their chases.
- If your feeders attract ants, coat the hanging string or wire with a thin coat of petroleum jelly. But keep grease off the feeders. If grease gets on the birds' feathers, it could harm them seriously.
- If only one hummer comes to your large feeder, separate the feeder into four smaller feeders. Place them around your yard where vegetation hides one from the others. If your feeder is in a hummer's territory, the hummer may try to keep other hummers from visiting. Having more than one feeder up gives the other hummers a chance to feed.

or hang each feeder in a different part of your yard.

Don't forget! Every two or three days in warm weather and every five days in cold weather, clean your feeders in a solution of 1 part liquid bleach and 10 parts water.

10:1

CAUTION! The bleach solution should be prepared with the help of an adult. Bleach is a dangerous chemical that can burn your skin and ruin your clothes if spilled.

Cleaning the Feeders

Bacteria and mold that could be harmful to hummers tend to build up in feeders. Your feeders *must* be cleaned at least every three days in warm weather—above 65°F (18°C)—and every five days in cool weather. If the nectar solution becomes cloudy, the feeders must be cleaned immediately. Here's how:

1. Take the feeders down, separate them if they are connected together, and dispose of any remaining liquid. *Never add new nectar solution to the remaining old solution.*

2. Pop the cups out of the bases. Have an adult help you soak the feeders for about a half hour in a solution of 1 part liquid bleach and 10 parts water. *Do not use any kind of soap or detergent.*

3. If mold has started to grow inside a feeder, after soaking the feeder dip a pipe cleaner in some of the bleach solution and use the pipe cleaner to scrub the hard-to-reach parts of the feeder. *Be sure you remove all the mold.*

4. Rinse all parts of the feeders thoroughly with hot water. Refill the feeders with new nectar solution and hang them back up for the hummers.

Why Aren't Hummingbirds Coming to My Feeders?

- Sugar solution left in a feeder for a while can start to ferment—turn into alcohol—and then hummingbirds will not feed on it. When you first hang your feeders, fill them only partway with nectar. As more hummers arrive, you can increase the amount of nectar to keep up with the demand.

- You may live in an area that does not have many flowers, trees, or shrubs that hummers like. Planting more such plants in your garden will help (see "Plant a Hummingbird Garden" on pages 34 to 35).

- During migration, it's not uncommon to have quite a few hummers around, but as nesting gets underway, their numbers tend to drop. Females are keeping their eggs warm or feeding young, and many males have moved to areas where a fresh wildflower bloom is taking place. When the young begin to fly, they may come to your feeder with the adult females.

- It can take a few days or even weeks to attract your first hummingbird, but once hummers have discovered your feeder, they will return to it year after year.

WHEN SHOULD I TAKE MY FEEDERS DOWN?

Take your feeders down after the last hummers have gone. Clean the feeders carefully before storing them. If you're lucky enough to live in an area that has hummers year-round, you may leave your feeders up throughout the year.

Start a field notebook in which to keep records of the hummers that visit your yard and your results for the hummer experiments.

Hummingbird Projects

Document Your Hummingbirds' Arrival

Keep a record of when the different species of hummers arrive in your area. Note whether the birds you see are male or female. Hummingbirds have what *ornithologists*—scientists who study birds—call a *differential migration*, meaning that the males arrive on the breeding grounds before the females. Males can arrive up to three weeks before the females. Also note the wildflowers that are blooming in your area when the hummers appear. In future years, when you see these flowers blooming, you'll know the hummers will soon be back!

Keeping records year after year is fun. See how close to the same day each year the birds arrive in and leave your area.

Provide Nesting Materials for Your Hummers

Gather some down from plants such as cattail (*Typha* spp.), willow (*Salix* spp.), and cottonwood (*Populus* spp.), and place it in a mesh bag—the type onions often come in. Hang the bag in your yard near your feeders. Hummers may gather the plant down for their nests. Keep track of which materials your hummingbirds prefer.

How Do Hummingbirds Control Their Temperatures?

Birds fluff up their feathers to help them trap and conserve body heat when it is cold. They press their feathers flat to their bodies to help release heat when it is warm. When hummers cannot release heat fast enough through their feathers, they cool themselves by panting and by hanging their legs and feet, with toes extended, away from their bodies. On cool days, they conserve heat by pulling their feet up into their feathers.

When hummers visit your feeder, make a note of the position of their feet and the temperature outside. Watch for hummers with their feet pulled right up into their feathers (their feet may not even show), hummers with their feet partially showing, and those with their feet fully extended and clearly visible.

In a similar study, ornithologists found that at temperatures

One look at this "flying thermometer" can tell you that the temperature is over 91°F (33°C).

above 91°F (33°C), Rufous and Allen's Hummingbirds extended their feet fully, but at temperatures of around 68°F (20°C) and below, they pulled their feet up into their feathers. How do your results compare with these?

Plant a Hummingbird Garden

You can provide additional food for your hummers by planting flowers especially for them—anywhere from a hanging basket on an apartment balcony to a flower bed in a backyard. In a yard, you can also provide your hummers with some shallow water for bathing and with trees or shrubs to give them protection from the weather, suitable perches, and nesting sites.

Hummingbirds will visit flowers of all sizes, colors, and shapes. They get nectar wherever they can. But some species of flowers have evolved with hummers, and these produce lots of nectar for long periods of time. Hummingbird flowers usually have tubular petals and are scentless (so they do not attract insects), brightly colored, and easy to hover at.

In your hummingbird garden, try to plant flowers that

Plants that give hummingbirds nectar get something from the hummers in return. When a hummingbird sticks its bill into a blossom, yellow or white pollen from the flower collects on the bill, the hummer's face, and the top of its head. When the hummer moves to another flower, some of the pollen rubs off, *pollinating*, or fertilizing, the flower.

bloom at different times of the year. Plant the flowers according to their size, with the taller varieties at the back and the smaller plants near the front.

Annual flowers are ideal for container gardens. They usually have lots of blossoms and bloom for a long time. Many flowering vines are also great for attracting hummers.

Most hummers will start nesting about a month after they arrive, so try to have your hummer garden in bloom before then. Once the birds establish themselves in an area, it's not likely that they will move long distances to new food sources, even though your yard may have a great hummingbird garden. Pesticides and herbicides should be avoided in a hummingbird garden.

Here are some common hummingbird flowers to try. Most of them grow throughout much of North America, but check to make sure they will do well where you live. Your local nursery will be able to help you.

ANNUALS
flowering sages (*Salvia* sp.)
foxglove (*Digitalis purpurea*)
gladiolus (*Gladiolus* hybr.)
impatiens and jewelweed
 (*Impatiens* hybr.)
nasturtium (*Tropaeolum majus*)
snapdragon (*Antirrhinum majus*)

PERENNIALS
bee balm (*Monarda didyma*)
bleeding heart (*Dicentra* sp.)
butterflyweed
 (*Asclepias tuberosa*)
cardinal flower
 (*Lobelia cardinalis*)
columbine (*Aquilegia* sp.)
delphinium and larkspur
 (*Delphinium* sp.)
fuchsia (*Fuchsia* sp.)
monkey flower (*Mimulus* sp.)
paintbrush (*Castilleja* sp.)
penstemon (*Penstemon* sp.)
phlox (*Phlox* sp.)
pinks (*Silene* sp.)

VINES & SHRUBS
fuchsia (*Fuchsia* sp.)
honeysuckle (*Lonicera* sp.)
morning glory (*Ipomoea* sp.)
red-flowering currant (*Ribes* sp.)
trumpet creeper
 (*Campsis radicans*)
winter jasmine
 (*Jasminum nudiflorum*)

Feeder Experiments

Do hummingbirds have a favorite color? Can they learn? How sweet do they like their nectar? In the following experiments, based on experiments conducted by ornithologists, you'll find out!

Instructions

For each experiment, you will need:
- your four hummingbird feeders
- white granulated sugar and water
- a place to hang the four feeders in a row—about 8 inches (20 cm) apart and all at the same height from the ground. The background should be the same for all four feeders.
- a notebook.

Ornithologists have found that hummingbirds learn and remember the position of a feeder quickly. In each of the following experiments, you will hang the four feeders in four different orders so that each feeder hangs once in each

position. In this way, you will eliminate the importance of position from each experiment.

For each experiment, you will record 25 hummer feeding sessions for each color order (100 sessions in all).

1. Read the instructions for the feeder experiment and fill the feeders according to the instructions.

2. In a notebook, make a chart to record the feeding sessions for each arrangement of feeders (see "Experiment Charts" on page 38).

3. Hang the feeders in Color Order A: ■ ■ ■ ■.

4. When a hummingbird arrives at the feeders, record on your chart how many times the hummer visits each of the feeders before it leaves. Do this for 25 different feeding sessions.

5. Rehang the feeders in Color Order B: ■ ■ ■ ■. Record 25 more feeding sessions.

6. Rehang the feeders in Color Order C: ■ ■ ■ ■. Record 25 more feeding sessions.

7. Rehang the feeders in Color Order D: ■ ■ ■ ■. Record 25 more feeding sessions.

8. Add up all the visits for each color.

You don't have to make all the observations at one time. You can observe at random times throughout the day or over a week. You can record many visits from the same hummer. Just be sure that each feeder has some liquid showing when you make your observations.

FEEDER EXPERIMENT CHARTS

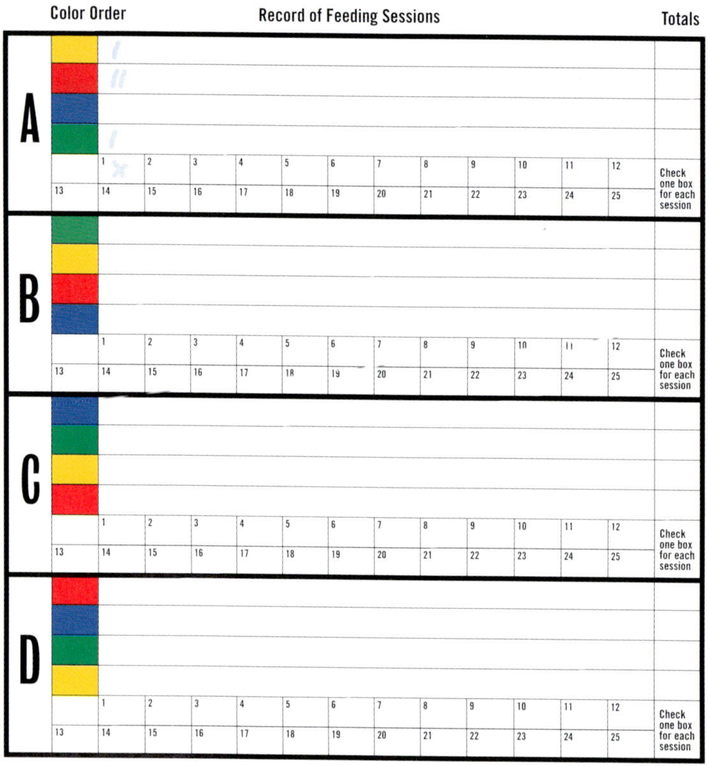

Here's how to record each hummingbird feeding session. If a hummer arrives and begins feeding at the 🟥 feeder, then moves to the 🟦 feeder, then to the 🟨 feeder, then back to the 🟥 feeder, then flies off, that would be one feeding session, and you would record four feeder visits, as shown on the sample chart.

Each time you record a feeding session, be sure to cross out one of the 25 boxes on the chart, so that you don't lose count.

When you have recorded 25 feeding sessions for each of the four color orders, on a chart like the one below, add up all visits for each color.

You can enlarge these charts on a color photocopier or draw your own charts in your notebook.

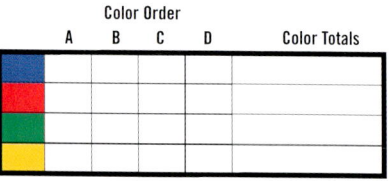

EXPERIMENT 1
Do Hummingbirds Have a Favorite Color?

- Mix some sugar solution (*4 parts water to 1 part white granulated sugar—see page 26*) and fill each feeder.
- Record 25 feeding sessions for each of the four color orders, for a total of 100 sessions. Then add up the visits for each of the four colors.

If the totals are all about the same, you could reasonably conclude that hummingbirds don't have a favorite color. However, since the shape of the feeders and the sugar solution in each feeder is the same, if one feeder has many more visits than the rest, it is likely that your hummingbirds prefer its color.

In similar experiments, ornithologists have found that hummingbirds do not appear to have a color preference—even for red!

Hummers may seem to be attracted to red flowers because many kinds of red flowers produce a lot of nectar. Red does not attract the attention of insects that feed on nectar. Red also stands out well against the green foliage, making it a likely place to search for food.

It appears that red is an indicator to hummingbirds that there may be food available, so they check it out. Thus, while hummers captured by ornithologists at red flowers and then given a choice of feeder colors picked red feeders to feed at, those captured at yellow flowers chose yellow feeders.

EXPERIMENT 2
Can Hummingbirds Learn?

- Mix some sugar solution (*4 parts water to 1 part white granulated sugar—see page 26*) and fill the yellow feeder only.
- Fill the other feeders with plain water.
- Record 25 feeding sessions for each of the four color orders, for a total of 100 sessions. Then add up the visits for each of the four colors.

If the totals are all about the same, it is likely that your hummingbirds had trouble learning that the yellow feeder was the only feeder that contained sugar solution. However, if the yellow feeder had many more visits than the rest, since each feeder was placed in every position, and the only obvious difference between the feeders is their color, it is likely that the hummingbirds learned that it was the yellow feeder that contained the sugar solution.

Ornithologists have found that hummers are able to learn by using visual clues. This ability enables the hummers to learn and remember the location of flower patches from one year to the next, and which flowers they have visited recently and emptied of nectar, thus ensuring that they don't waste more energy hovering than they get back from the nectar in the flowers.

EXPERIMENT 3
How Sweet Do Hummingbirds Like Their Nectar?

- Make up four different sugar solutions (*see page 26*) as follows:

- 🟦 1 part sugar to 1 part water
- 🟨 1 part sugar to 2 parts water
- 🟩 1 part sugar to 4 parts water
- 🟥 1 part sugar to 8 parts water
- Record 25 feeding sessions for each of the four color orders, for a total of 100 sessions. Then add up the visits for each of the four colors.

If the total number of visits for each sugar concentration is about the same, it would suggest that your hummingbirds don't have a favorite concentration. However, since each feeder was placed in every position, the feeders are the same shape, and you have determined that the hummers do not have a favorite color—but they can learn from the color which feeder has the higher concentration—then, if one concentration has many more visits than the rest, your hummers likely prefer that concentration.

Ornithologists have found that hummingbirds do prefer a high sugar concentration, which offers more energy for less effort as hummers strive to meet their high energy needs.

> **NOTE!**
> The sugar concentration of the nectar that hummers normally feed on is in the range of 1:5 to 1:4. Feeding hummingbirds on a higher sugar concentration while you conduct this short experiment will probably have little effect on them. After completing this experiment, however, it is important for the health of the hummers to keep the sugar solution you regularly feed them at around 1 part sugar to 4 parts water.

Field Guide

Identifying Hummingbirds

Each hummingbird species is different. Ornithologists look at a hummer's outer parts for clues to the bird's identity. They also listen to the sounds the bird makes and observe its behavior. These features are called *field marks*. Female and young hummingbirds of nearly all species are very difficult to identify because they look so much alike. Here are some things to look for:

Color: Note the colors on the hummer's back, crown, throat, bill, and underparts. These are often the best (and only) field marks you can see.

Wings: The wings of some hummers are longer than the tail, making the tail look pointed when the bird is perched.

Undersides: Many species are very drab underneath, but some have obvious *buffy* (dull yellow) undersides or have buffy or greenish coloration on the flanks.

Tail: Can you see any patterns, spots, or white on the outer tail feathers? Also look at the color of the underside of the tail. Is the tail notched (forked)?

Bill: What is the length of the bill in relation to the bird's overall size? Is the bill curved or straight? Is it colored or black?

Sounds: What voice or feather sounds can you hear?

Behavior: When feeding, does the hummer flip or spread its tail? What is the pattern of its flight display? (See pages 17 to 19.)

Size: Identifying a single hummer by size is difficult, but comparing the size of two or more at the same time can be very helpful.

Distribution: Use the distribution maps beside the species illustrations to identify which species frequent your area. Always be alert for a hummingbird far from its normal range—it will be a special find.

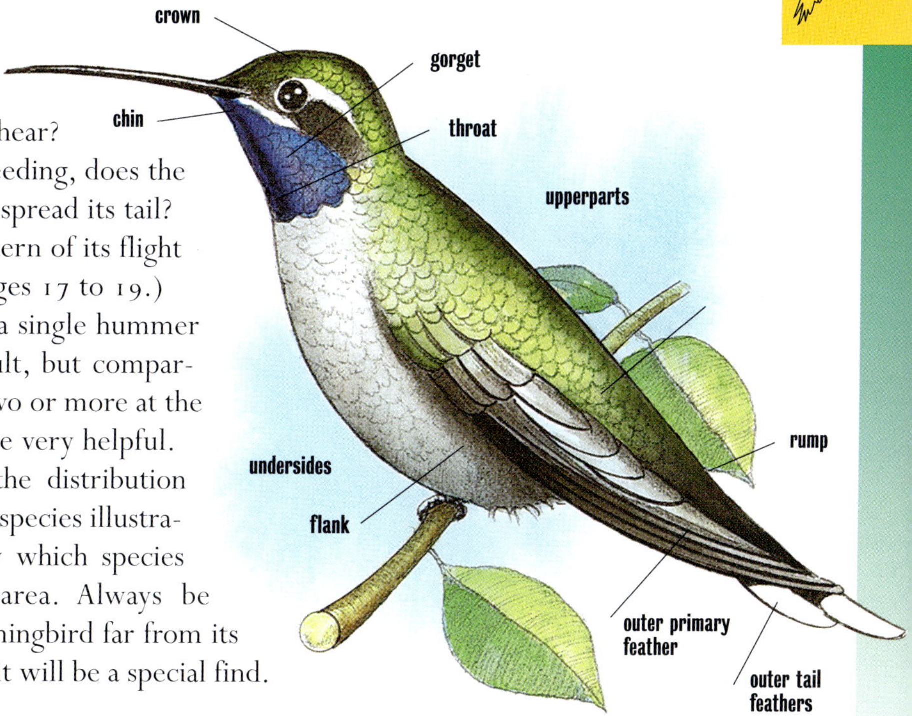

RUBY-THROATED HUMMINGBIRD
(*Archilochus colubris*)

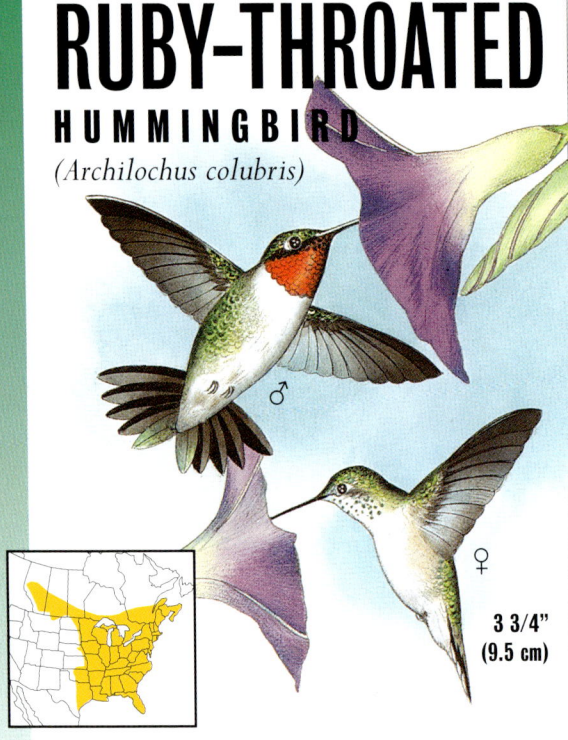

3 3/4"
(9.5 cm)

Field Marks: *Male:* Metallic green upperparts, whitish undersides with greenish sides and flanks, ruby-red throat, black chin, the black extending to below the eye, deeply forked tail with green center and black sides. *Female:* Greenish upperparts, green forehead, whitish undersides and throat, buffy flanks, rounded tail with white spots.

Sounds: High-pitched, mouselike, squeaky *zzzt-zzz*, or a *tchew* call.

Habitat: Mixed and deciduous woods, parks, and backyard gardens.

Field Notes: The Ruby-throat is the only hummingbird that regularly occurs and breeds in the eastern half of North America. During migration, it crosses the Gulf of Mexico, a nonstop flight of more than 500 miles (800 km). Traveling at an average speed of around 25 miles per hour (40 km/hr), the Ruby-throat takes about 20 hours of nonstop flying to complete the journey.

Some Ruby-throats have a close association with sapsuckers—they feed regularly on the sap and insects at sapsucker wells in trees.

3 3/4"
(9.5 cm)

BLACK-CHINNED HUMMINGBIRD
(Archilochus alexandri)

Field Marks: *Male:* Dark green upperparts, olive-green sides, white collar, and black chin bordered on lower throat by iridescent purple, slightly notched dark tail. *Female:* Iridescent green upperparts, white undersides, lacks any *rufous* (rusty red) on tail. *Both:* Small white spot behind eyes, bill slightly downturned, tail constantly flipped and spread while bird hovers.

Sounds: A distinct, descending, soft *chew* or *teew;* also a chase call of high, buzzy notes. In flight, the male's wing feathers give a distinctive dry *buzz.*

Habitat: Oak and riparian woodlands, chaparrals, and urban parks and yards.

Field Notes: Like other northern hummers, Black-chinned Hummingbirds can be found in the lowlands early in the nesting season. However, by July, many of them have moved to higher elevations to feed on the mountain wildflowers that bloom later in the season.

Like other hummingbirds, the Black-chinned will sit on a conspicuous perch and, when an insect flies by, will dart out and catch it, flycatcher style.

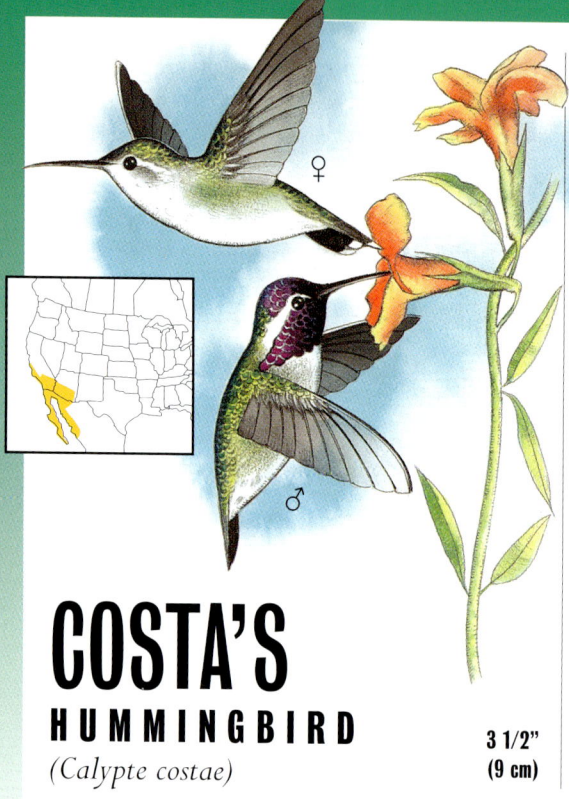

COSTA'S
HUMMINGBIRD
(Calypte costae)

3 1/2"
(9 cm)

Field Marks: *Male:* Green back, light gray undersides, purple gorget and crown. *Female:* Grayish-green upperparts, white undersides, some green wash on the flanks, no obvious buffy coloration underneath, no rufous on the tail, thin white line behind eye, unmarked (usually), white throat. *Both:* Stocky look, short and rounded tail that is often flipped up and down when feeding, wing tips extend beyond tail when perched, bill is slightly downcurved and thin.

Sounds: Call is a faint, high, metallic *chick, pit, tsik,* or *tink,* often given as a rapid twitter. In display flight, the male also gives a loud, high-pitched whistle, the pitch rising then falling. The sound has been compared to the *zing* of a ricocheting bullet.

Habitat: Arid regions such as deserts, chaparrals, and sagebrush areas.

Field Notes: Costa's Hummingbirds live in desert scrub. This hummer hasn't adapted to living closely with people. To meet its energy needs from flowers alone, the Costa's has to visit over 1,800 blossoms each day.

ANNA'S HUMMINGBIRD
(Calypte anna)

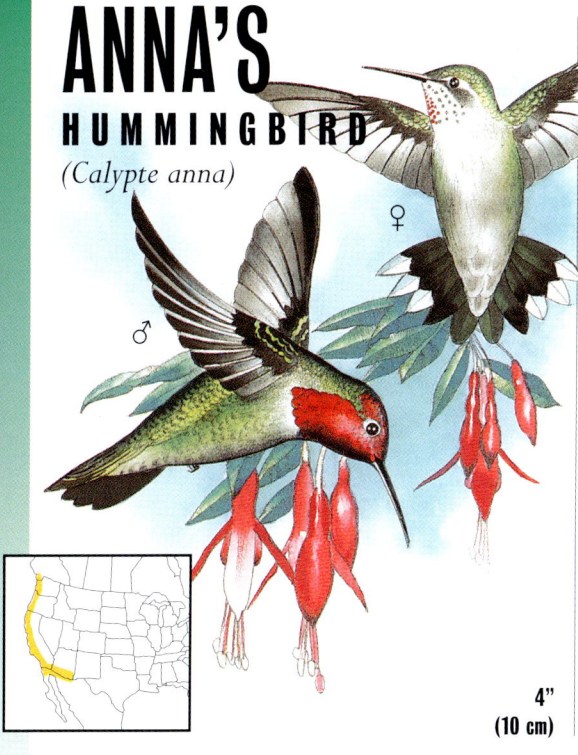

4"
(10 cm)

Field Marks: *Male:* Only North American hummer with rosy-red crown, also with a red throat, iridescent bronze-green upperparts, gray-green undersides. *Female:* Greenish upperparts, dirty gray undersides, lacks obvious buff, center of female's throat usually has some red spots, lacks red on crown, no rufous in tail. *Both:* Relatively short bill, when feeding the tail is held in line with body—it is seldom fanned or flipped up.

Sounds: One of the few hummingbirds with a "song." The male gives a series of coarse squeaks either from a noticeable perch or at the start of the display flight— *bzz bzz bzz chur-ZWEE dzi! dzi!* Call is a *chit, chirp,* or *che-che-che*.

Habitat: Mixed woods, chaparrals, canyons, bottomlands, and urban parks and gardens.

Field Notes: After feeding, the Anna's Hummingbird usually flies to an exposed perch and preens or turns its head from side to side. This hummer may begin nesting as early as December in California and as early as February in British Columbia.

CALLIOPE HUMMINGBIRD
(Stellula calliope)

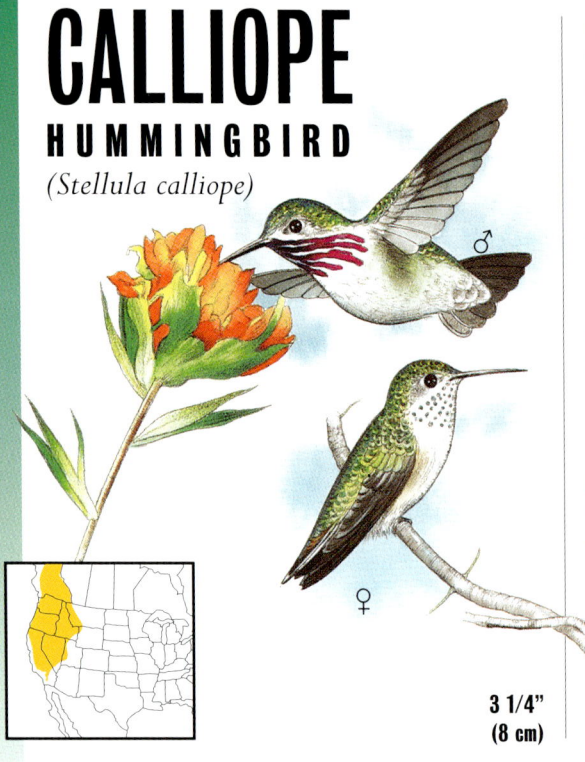

3 1/4"
(8 cm)

Field Marks: *Male:* Iridescent green upperparts, white undersides, greenish sides, brownish-gray tail, only hummer with a purple-red gorget that forms streaks against a white throat. *Female:* Green upperparts, whitish undersides, buffy sides, finely spotted throat, some rufous at base of tail. *Both:* Relatively short bill, stubby tail.

Sounds: Normally quite silent. Call is a high-pitched *tsew* or very thin *chip* or *tsip.* Males give a low *bzzt* when displaying.

Habitat: Mountainous regions, shrub areas including riparian thickets, mountain meadows and burns, lowland and subalpine meadows, aspen groves, and the edges and openings of coniferous forests.

Field Notes: The Calliope Hummer rarely flies more than 5 feet (1.5 m) above the ground. In mountainous areas, where night temperatures drop to near freezing, Calliope males go into torpor, dropping their body temperatures about 50°F (10°C). Incubating females, however, rely on protected nest sites and downy nest materials to help them and the eggs stay warm through the cold nights. The Calliope is the smallest bird north of Mexico, weighing about as much as a penny.

4"
(10 cm)

BROAD-TAILED
HUMMINGBIRD
(Selasphorus platycercus)

Field Marks: *Male:* Green upperparts, whitish undersides, metallic red gorget, tail that is green in the center and purple-black on the outer feathers (sometimes edged with rufous). *Female:* Green upperparts, white undersides, touch of buff on sides, small amount of rufous at base of outer tail feathers.

Sounds: Call is a clear *chip* or *chitter* often given in succession. The male's outer primary feathers are notched and make a very shrill *buzz* or trill in direct flight, as well as during display, as air rushes through the tapered tips of the feathers. This sound is used by the hummer to defend its territory. The outer primary feathers wear down so that by midwinter the trill is often no longer heard.

Habitat: Mountain meadows, shrub thickets, and edges of coniferous forests.

Field Notes: When male Broad-tailed hummers are defending a territory, they feed only lightly during the day. Scientists think they do this to keep themselves light and thus more maneuverable against other hummingbirds that try to move into their area.

RUFOUS
HUMMINGBIRD
(Selasphorus rufous)

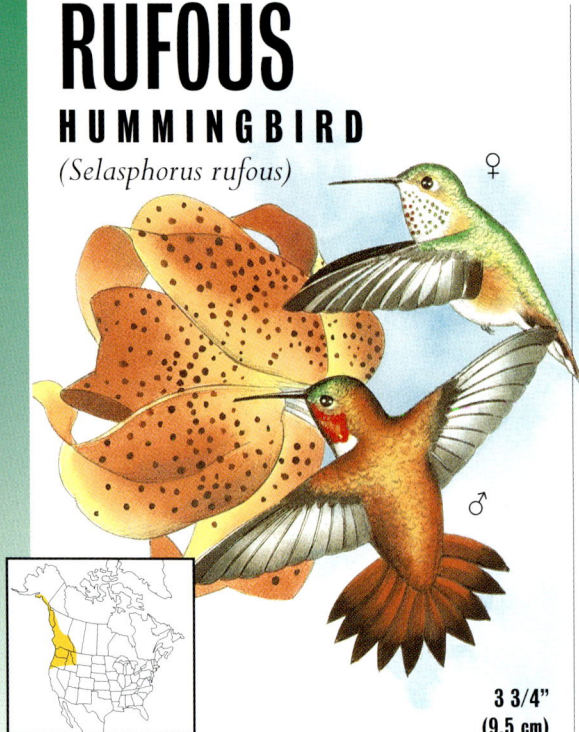

3 3/4"
(9.5 cm)

Field Marks: *Male:* Greenish head, extensive rufous coloring on back, sides, and tail, bright orange-red gorget. *Female:* Greenish upperparts, rufous on sides and base of tail, white tips on outer tail feathers, spotted throat, whitish undersides.

Sounds: Metallic whistle of the male's wings made both in display and direct flight. Gives a fast series of calls described as *eeeeee, didayer, didayer, didayer* or *zippity, zippity, zippity*. Both sexes have a warning *chip, chip, chip*.

Habitat: Lowland coniferous forests and deciduous woodlands, riparian thickets, orchards, and mountain meadows, as well as urban parks and gardens.

Field Notes: The Rufous Hummingbird has the widest distribution of all the hummingbirds in North America. It can outfly all other hummers and is perhaps the most aggressive in defending its territory. During migration, the Rufous has been known to take over and feed at established territories of other hummers. The spotted pattern on the female's throat is unique and can be used to identify different individuals visiting your feeders.

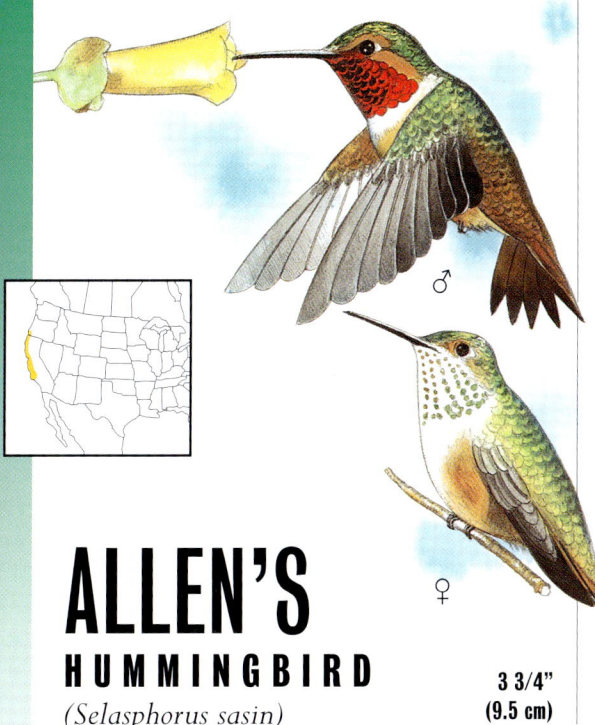

Field Marks: *Male:* Metallic bronze-green upperparts, rufous sides, rump, and tail, whitish undersides, orange-red throat. *Female:* Indistinguishable from female Rufous Hummingbird.

Sounds: Call is a hisslike *chup,* often one after another. The Allen's Hummingbird also has a chase note described as *zeee-chuppity-chup.* The male's wings produce a high, trilling rattle similar to that of the Rufous Hummer.

Habitat: Woodlands near damp ravines and canyons, chaparrals, mountain meadows, and open coniferous forests.

Field Notes: The wings of the Allen's Hummingbird move at about 40 beats per second in forward flight and while hovering.

An Allen's Hummer has been seen chasing a Red-tailed Hawk—a bird that weighs more than 330 times the weight of the little Allen's—away from its territory.

The Allen's has a special subspecies that lives on the Channel Islands off the California coast. These birds, like the Anna's Hummingbird, do not migrate.

ALLEN'S
HUMMINGBIRD
(Selasphorus sasin)

3 3/4"
(9.5 cm)

SOUTHWESTERN HUMMINGBIRDS

BROAD-BILLED HUMMINGBIRD: *Male:* Dark metallic green upperparts, breast, and belly, whitish under tail, forked blue-black tail, metallic blue-green throat, white spot behind eye. *Female:* Greenish upperparts, grayish undersides, unmarked gray throat, thin white line behind eye, gray ear patch below line. *Both:* Slightly downcurved, reddish bill with dark lip. *Occurs:* SW AZ, SW NM, and S Central TX.

WHITE-EARED HUMMINGBIRD: *Male:* Purple crown and throat. *Female:* Black ear patch below eye line, green spots on throat, bill not as bright red as the male's. *Both:* Mainly green, white line behind eye, red bill with dark tip. *Occurs:* SE AZ and SW NM, occasionally in S Central AZ.

VIOLET-CROWNED HUMMINGBIRD: *Male:* White throat and lacks typical gorget. *Female:* Crown less brilliant than the male's. *Both:* Blue-violet crown, white undersides, red bill with black tip. *Occurs:* SE and S Central AZ, SW NM.

BLUE-THROATED HUMMINGBIRD: *Male:* Metallic green upperparts, blue-gray undersides, two white lines on face, blue throat. *Female:* Green upperparts, even gray undersides, white line behind eye. *Both:* Large white tips on outer tail feathers. *Occurs:* SE AZ, SW NM, SW TX.

MAGNIFICENT HUMMINGBIRD: *Male:* Greenish upperparts, iridescent purple crown, metallic green throat, green-black breast, square tail has green-bronze feathers with gray tips. *Female:* Green upperparts, grayish underparts, spotted gray throat, green tail has outer tail feathers with gray tips. *Both:* Tiny white spot behind eye. *Occurs:* SE and Central AZ, occasionally in SW NM and SW TX.

LUCIFER HUMMINGBIRD: *Male:* Green upperparts, whitish undersides, purple gorget extending down sides of neck, buffy sides, deeply forked tail that at rest may appear pointed. *Female:* Green upperparts, deep-buffy undersides, light streak running from behind eye, outer tail feathers have rufous coloration near base. *Both:* Long downcurved bill. *Occurs:* Extreme SW TX, occasionally in SE AZ.

4"
(10 cm)

BROAD-BILLED
HUMMINGBIRD
(Cynanthus latirostris)

WHITE-EARED
HUMMINGBIRD
(Hylocharis leucotis)

3 1/2"
(9 cm)

VIOLET-CROWNED
HUMMINGBIRD
(Amazilia violiceps)

4 1/2"
(11.5 cm)

5"
(12.5 cm)

BLUE-THROATED
HUMMINGBIRD
(Lampornis clemenciae)

MAGNIFICENT
HUMMINGBIRD
(Eugenes fulgens)

5 1/4"
(13.5 cm)

3 1/2"
(9 cm)

LUCIFER
HUMMINGBIRD
(Calothorax lucifer)

Scientific Names

There are more than 100 billion birds on Earth—swimming birds, wading birds, diving birds, birds of prey, and perching birds—from more than 9,000 species. A single kind of bird often has many different names. The Ruby-throated Hummingbird is known as the Common Hummingbird in some areas. In French, its name is *Colibri à gorge rubis.*

To avoid confusion, scientists classify each kind of living thing by giving it a scientific name that is the same throughout the world. The name usually comes from Latin, a language no longer spoken. Scientific names are set in italic type and consist of two parts: the genus and the species name. First, scientists divide living things into five kingdoms. The two most familiar are the animal and plant kingdoms. Everything in each group is then divided and grouped further right down to individual species. Here, for example, is how scientists classify the Ruby-throated Hummingbird:

Kingdom: Animalia (animals)
Phylum: Chordata (vertebrates)
Class: Aves (birds)
Order: Apodiformes (swifts and hummingbirds)
Family: Trochilidae (hummingbirds)
Genus: *Archilochus*
Species: *colubris*